HORRID HENRY'S JOLLY JOKE BOOK

Francesca Simon spent her childhood on the beach in California, and then went to Yale and Oxford Universities to study medieval history and literature. She now lives in London with her English husband and their son. When she is not writing books she is doing theatre and restaurant reviews or chasing after her Tibetan Spaniel, Shanti.

Tony Ross is one of Britain's best known illustrators, with many picture books to his name as well as line drawings for many fiction titles.

Also by Francesca Simon

Don't Cook Cinderella
Helping Hercules

and for younger readers

Mr P's Naughty Book
The Parent Swap Shop
Spider School
The Topsy-Turvies

HORRID HENRY'S JOLLY JOKE BOOK

Francesca Simon

Illustrated by Tony Ross

Orion
Children's Books

ORION CHILDREN'S BOOKS

First published in Great Britain in 2007 by Orion Children's Books
This reissued edition first published in 2008
This edition published in 2016 by Hodder and Stoughton

12

Text copyright © Francesca Simon, 2007
Illustrations copyright © Tony Ross, 2007

A CIP catalogue record for this book
is available from the British Library.

ISBN 978 1 4072 2755 9

Printed and bound in Great Britain
by Clays Ltd, St Ives plc

The paper and board used in this book are
made from wood from responsible sources.

Orion Children's Books
An imprint of
Hachette Children's Group
Part of Hodder and Stoughton
Carmelite House
50 Victoria Embankment
London EC4Y 0DZ

An Hachette UK Company
www.hachette.co.uk

www.hachettechildrens.co.uk

Acknowledgements

Many thanks to the children of
Avondale Park Primary School
and High Ham School, who told
me some great jokes. And special
thanks to Charlotte Mendelson for
the "interrupting sheep" joke,
and to Kate Ballard.

CONTENTS

HORRiD HENRY'S JOLLY JOKE BOOK

Bleeeeeeccchhhh! What a bunch of copycats! Miss Battle-Axe said everyone in the school could put their best jokes in this new joke book, and the person with the best one would get a really, really great prize. Whoopee! Well, let them try to out-joke me. My Purple Hand Pirate jokes are sure to be the best. Margaret wouldn't know a good joke if it banged her over the head. And as for Peter - no way is he wrecking this book with his stupid worm toad jokes.

Henry, this is a school joke book and I have just as much right to put in my jokes as you do.

Says who?

Says Miss Lovely.

We'll see about that. I'm the boss and what I say goes.

Oh Yeah? Says who?

Says me, Margaret, you old pants face.

No one made you boss, Henry. And your jokes are stupid.

**Not as stupid as yours.
Vote Henry! Vote Henry! Vote Henry!**

FIONA'S FIERY FANGMANGLER JOKES

My jokes are
the best! Vote Fiona!!

NO! Vote Henry!!

Shut up, Henry.

Shut up yourself!

*What's a shark's
favourite game?*
Bite and seek.

Why didn't the skeleton go swimming?
Because he had no body to go with.

What do devils drink?
Demonade.

*What's a monster's
favourite soup?*
Scream of tomato.

What did one cool ghost say to the other?
Get a life, dude.

Who is green and eats porridge?
Mouldy Locks.

What did the cannibal say when he came home and found his mum chopping up a python and a pygmy?

'Oh no, not snake and pygmy pie again!'

Why should you stay calm when you meet a cannibal?
Because it's no good getting in a stew.

What does a cannibal call a phone book?
A menu.

Why did the cannibal go to the wedding reception?
So he could toast the guests.

What did the cannibal say when he saw
Graham asleep?
'Aaaaah! Breakfast in bed.'

**Pssst! Everyone. Just skip ahead
to my pirate jokes! Vote Henry!**

ANDREW'S ANXIOUS JOKES

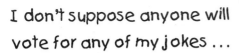

I don't suppose anyone will vote for any of my jokes ...

What do you call an anxious dinosaur?
A nervous rex.

PSYCHIATRIST: What's your problem?
PATIENT: I think I'm a chicken.
PSYCHIATRIST: How long has this been going on?
PATIENT: Ever since I was an egg.

What's the worst vegetable to have on a boat?
A leek.

What lies at the bottom of the ocean and twitches?
A nervous wreck.

GURINDER'S GORGEOUS JOKES

I'm the most beautiful girl in the class, so I deserve to win.

Yeah, right, Gurinder. Not!

GURINDER: I spend hours in front of the mirror admiring myself. Do you think that's vanity?
MARGARET: No, imagination.

MARGARET: My beauty is timeless.
GURINDER: Yeah, it could stop a clock.

GURINDER: Will I lose my looks when I get older?
MARGARET: With luck, yes.

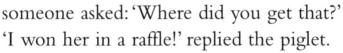

A blonde was walking down the road with a piglet under her arm. As she passed the school, someone asked: 'Where did you get that?' 'I won her in a raffle!' replied the piglet.

Why was the girl named Sugar?
Because she was so refined.

How does a blonde kill a fish?
She drowns it.

Did you hear about the blonde tap dancer? She fell in the sink.

What did Snow White say while she waited for her photos?
Some day my prints will come.

What did the stamp say to the envelope on Valentine's Day?
I'm stuck on you.

What did one magnet say to the other magnet?
I find you very attractive.

What do you call a girl with sausages on her head?
Barbie.

I don't think these photographs you've taken do me justice.
You don't want justice – you want mercy.

NICK: Do you think my sister Lily is pretty?
HENRY: Well, let's just say if you pulled her pigtail she'd probably say 'oink, oink.'

Vote Gurinder!

MARGARET'S MOODY JOKES

I think I'll help Margaret with a few jokes . . .

What's the difference between Margaret and a cow?

Nothing, they're both Moooooooooooooooooooooooooooooooody.

Oy, Henry, quit pretending to be me. I'm
not putting in moody jokes, so there. I've
got a much better idea.

Oh yeah?

Yeah. Ha ha ha.

SUSAN'S SOUR JOKES

SUSAN: I always use lemon juice for my complexion.
MARGARET: Maybe that's why you always looks so sour.

What's the difference between Susan and Starbursts?
Nothing. They're both sour.

SUSAN: Boys whisper they love me.
HENRY: Well, they wouldn't admit it out loud, would they?

Hey, I didn't write those!

I wrote them for you, Susan – tee hee.

Who won the monster beauty contest?
No one.

They say Margaret is a raving beauty.
You mean she's escaped from the funny farm?

Henry went into a joke store . . . and saw himself.

You mean Susan went into a joke store . . .

Why are Susan and a snake alike?
They're ssssssssssour.

MARGARET'S ABOMINABLE SNOWMAN JOKES

Hey, that's not fair! Margaret should put in moody jokes NOT snowman jokes.

Too bad, Henry! Now I'm sure to win. Vote Margaret!

What did Jack Frost say to Frosty the Snowman?
Have an ice day.

PATIENT: Doctor, doctor, I keep thinking I'm a snowman.
DOCTOR: Keep cool.

Where does a snowman put his birthday candles?
On his birthday flake.

What do snowmen wear on their heads?
Ice caps.

What do you get if you cross a snowman and a shark?
Frostbite.

Where do snowmen put their webpages?
On the winternet.

What do snowmen call their offspring?
Chill–dren.

What happened when the icicle landed on the snowman's head?
It knocked him cold.

What did the snowman and his wife put over their baby's crib?
A snowmobile.

Where do snowmen go to dance?
To snowballs.

Why did a snowman send his father to Siberia?
Because he wanted frozen pop.

How does a snowman get to work?
By icicle.

What two letters of the alphabet do snowmen prefer?
I.C.

Where do snowmen keep their money?
In a snowbank.

What kind of money do snowmen use?
Ice lolly.

BOUDICCA'S BATTLE-AXE JOKES

I have always had an excellent sense of humour, so I feel it is my duty to share some of my favourite jokes with you. Anyone who does not vote one of my jokes the best in the book will get four hours of homework a night.

What was the greatest accomplishment of the early Romans?
Speaking Latin.

Why does history keep repeating itself?
Because we weren't listening the first time.

What does a library book wear whenever it leaves the building?
A pager.

What did the executioner say to his mother?
Only thirty chopping days to Christmas.

Why are soldiers so tired on April 1st?
They've just completed a
31 day March.

What did one knife say to the other?
Look sharp.

What sort of star is dangerous?
A shooting star.

Who invented King Arthur's round table?
Sir Cumference.

*When was King Arthur's army
too tired to fight?*
When they had too many
sleepless knights.

Why did Henry VIII have so many wives?
He liked to chop and change.

TEACHER JOKES

1 + 1 = 2

Pssst! Don't tell Miss Battle-Axe, but I've sneaked a few *real* teacher jokes into the book. Won't she get a shock!!!

MISS BATTLE-AXE: *If 1+1=2 and 2+2=4, what is 4+4?*

HENRY: That's not fair! You answer the easy ones and leave us with the hard one.

MISS BATTLE-AXE: Order! Order!

HENRY: I'll have some chocolates and crisps.

2 + 2 = 4

HENRY: Mum, I've got great news.

MUM: Did you pass your test?

HENRY: Nah, but I was top of those who failed.

$3 + 3 = 6$

MISS BATTLE-AXE: What's 2 and 2?

CLEVER CLARE: 4

MISS BATTLE-AXE: That's good.

CLEVER CLARE: Good? That's perfect!

What kind of food do maths teachers eat?
Square meals.

$4 + 4 = 8$

MISS BATTLE-AXE: Well, at least there's one thing I can say about Henry.

DAD: What's that?

MISS BATTLE-AXE: With grades like these, he couldn't be cheating.

27

MISS BATTLE-AXE: What do you call a person who keeps on talking when people are no longer interested?
HENRY: A teacher.

HENRY: Hey Dad, can you write in the dark?
DAD: What do you want me to write?
HENRY: Your name on this school report.

MISS BATTLE-AXE: If I had seven oranges in one hand and eight oranges in the other, what would I have?
HORRID HENRY: Big hands.

MR NERDON: Ralph, why are you doing your maths sums on the floor?

RUDE RALPH: You told me to do it without using tables.

MISS BATTLE-AXE: Henry, go to the map and find America.

HENRY: Here it is.

MISS BATTLE-AXE: Correct. Now, class, who discovered America?

CLASS: Henry.

MRS ODDBOD: Why are you late?

SOUR SUSAN: Because of the sign.

MRS ODDBOD: What sign?

SOUR SUSAN: The one that says, 'School Ahead, Go Slow'.

MISS BATTLE-AXE:
What's the chemical
formula for water?
HORRID HENRY:
HIJKLMNO.

MISS BATTLE-AXE:
What are you talking about?
HORRID HENRY: Yesterday you said
it's H to O.

MISS BATTLE-AXE: Why is your
homework in your father's handwriting?
HENRY: I used his pen.

MISS BATTLE-AXE: How can you
prevent diseases caused by biting
insects?
CLEVER CLARE: Don't bite any.

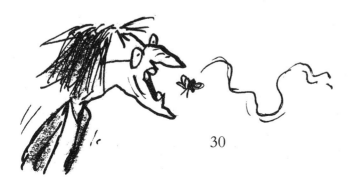

Have you heard about the teacher who was cross-eyed?
She couldn't control her pupils!

MISS BATTLE-AXE: Henry, your essay on 'My Cat' is exactly the same as Peter's. Did you copy his?

HORRID HENRY: No, it's the same cat.

MISS BATTLE-AXE: Where is your homework?

HENRY: I lost it fighting this kid who said you weren't the best teacher in the school.

Now if that doesn't win the prize for me . . . tee hee!

LINDA'S LAZY JOKES

Yawn. I'm too tired to tell any jokes ...

What should you do if you find a snake in your bed?
Sleep in the wardrobe.

LAZY LINDA: I don't think my mum knows much about children.

GORGEOUS GURINDER: Why do you say that?

LAZY LINDA: Because she always puts me to bed when I'm wide awake, and gets me up when I'm sleepy.

Why did the girl put her bed in the fireplace?
Because she wanted to sleep like a log.

How can you get breakfast in bed?
Sleep in the kitchen.

What's an undercover agent?
A spy in bed.

Where do books sleep?
Under their covers.

Why can't a bicycle stand up?
Because it's too tired.

Why shouldn't you believe a person in bed?
Because he is lying.

*How do you get
an alien baby to
sleep?*
You rock-et.

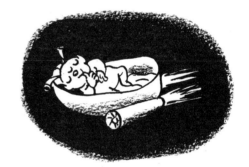

That's quite enough (yawn).

GRAHAM'S GREEDY JOKES

C'mon everybody, vote for one of mine!
I hear the prize is double your weight in
sweets! And I don't
get enough sweets.
I'm starving!
I need
chocolate!
I need
sweets! I'm
feeling weak
from lack of
sweets. These
jokes are making me
hungry ... Gimme sweeeeeets!!!!

Knock! Knock!
Who's there?
Ice cream!
Ice cream who?
*Ice cream if you throw
me in cold water.*

Knock! Knock!

Who's there?

Ice cream soda.

Icecreamsodawho?

*ICE CREAM SODA PEOPLE CAN
HEAR ME . . .*

How do you make a cream puff?
Chase it round the block.

Knock knock.
Who's there?
Stew.
Stew, who?
Stew early to go to bed.

How do you fix a broken pizza?
With tomato paste.

How did the burger propose?
With an onion ring.

Why do hamburgers go to the gym?
To get better buns.

What are two things you can't have for lunch?
Breakfast and dinner.

What country did sweets come from?
Sweeten.

What did the cake say to the knife?
You wanna piece of me?

What did the nut say when it sneezed?
Cashew.

What do you get if you cross a snake with a pie?
A pie-thon.

What do Italian monsters eat?
Spook-ghetti.

What is a pie's favorite sport?
Pie Kwan Do.

What did the teddy bear say when he was offered dessert?
No thanks, I'm stuffed!

THE FAMILY OF TOMATOES

A family of three tomatoes were walking in town one day when the baby tomato started lagging behind. The big father tomato walked back to the baby tomato, stomped on her, and said, 'Ketchup!'

What do you get when you cross a cocoa bean with an elk?
Chocolate moose.

Where did the spaghetti go to dance?
The meat-ball.

What's yellow and stupid?
Thick custard.

What do you call two banana peels?
A pair of slippers.

Waiter, waiter, this soup tastes funny.
Well, you did ask for something with a little body in it.

Why is 't' so important to a stick insect?
Because without it, it would be a sick insect.

Why did the banana go out with the prune?
He couldn't find a date.

What is yellow and white, and throws itself off the edge of the dining table?
A lemming meringue.

These jokes are making me starving! Vote Graham. I need sweets.

MARTHA'S MAGIC JOKES

Abracadabra, hocus pocus, when I count to three, you will all vote for me . . .

Nice try, Martha. But you can't beat my pirate jokes!

What happened to the magic tractor?
It went down the lane and turned into a field.

MISS BATTLE-AXE: What's your father's job?

MAGIC MARTHA: He's a magician.

MISS BATTLE-AXE: How interesting. What's his favourite trick?

MAGIC MARTHA: He saws people in half.

MISS BATTLE-AXE: Goodness. Do you have any brothers of sisters?

MAGIC MARTHA: One half brother and two half sisters.

Why can't the magician tell his magic secrets in the garden?
The corn has ears and the potatoes have eyes.

How did the magician cut the sea in half?
With a sea saw.

What do a footballer and a magician have in common?
Both do hat tricks.

You will all vote for me, you will all vote for me, you will all vote for me . . .

WILLIAM'S WEEPY JOKE

Waaaaahhh! I wanted to tell my joke first ...

Why was the cookie crying?
Because its mother had been a wafer so long.

Waaaahhh! Nobody laughed at my joke ...

SORAYA'S SINGING JOKES

Tra la la la la. Do re mi fa so la ti do. Do ti la so fa—

Oh shut up Soraya!

Miss Battle-Axe! Henry told me to shut up!

Don't be horrid, Henry, or I'll remove your jokes from the book.

Huh. She wouldn't dare . . .

What's the most musical part of a turkey?
The drumstick.

Why can't skeletons sing in church? Because they've got no organs.

What do you call a musical automobile?
A car—toon.

What is a monster's favourite song? Ghouls just want to have fun.

What kind of music does a mummy listen to? Wrap music.

Why did Miss Thumper get locked in a classroom?
Because her keys were in the piano.

What's green and sings?
Elvis Parsley.

*What's the most
musical bone?*
The trom–bone.

*What's the wettest animal in
the world?*
Reindeer.

What sugar sings?
Icing sugar.

Why did Mozart sell his sheep?
Because they wouldn't stop saying, 'Bach!
Bach!'

RALPH'S RUDE JOKES

Oh boy, stop reading now, all you prissy toads. These jokes are so rude—

Hey, that's not fair! I want to tell the rude jokes!

Too bad, Henry, I got here first.

I order you to stop. These are *my* jokes.

No way!

I told Ralph all these jokes anyway. So really they count as mine.

What did one toilet say to the other?
You look a bit flushed.

Why did Peter take toilet paper to the party?
Because he was a party pooper.

Hey, Ralph!
That's really funny.

No it isn't! Mum! Miss Lovely! Ralph called
me a party pooper!

Shut up, tell-tale.

*Why did the toilet roll roll down
the hill?*
It wanted to get to the
bottom.

Why do boys have spots?
So they can play dot to dot.

*What did the toilet roll say to the other toilet
roll?*
People keep ripping me off.

Doctor, doctor, I've got a sore throat.
So go over to the window and stick
your tongue out.
Why will that help?
It won't. I just don't like my
neighbours.

What tree can't you climb?
A lavatory.

What colour is a burp?
Burple.

What do you call a fairy who hasn't taken a bath?
Stinkerbell.

What does a queen bee do when she burps?
Issues a royal pardon.

Did you ever see the movie 'Constipated'?
It never came out.

*What did the judge say when the skunk
walked into the courtroom?*
Odour in the court.

*How do you know when a dog has been
naughty?*
It leaves a little poodle on the carpet.

What did one eye say to the other eye?
Just between you and me . . . something
smells.

What's brown and sounds like a bell?
Dung.

Knock knock.
 Who's there?
 The interrupting sheep.
The interrupting
sh—
BAAAAAA!

What do you get if you cross Henry and Margaret?
A mess.

That is so not funny, Ralph!
Yes it is, Henry.
Is not!

Is too!

Okay, what do you get if you cross Ralph and Margaret? A big mess.

That is <u>so</u> not funny, Henry!

AL'S AEROBIC JOKES

One-two, one-two, one-two, c'mon you lazy lumps, get out there, shake a leg, run ten miles, do some press-ups, climb a mountain, swim the Atlantic . . . Stop lying about! Put down this book and go for a run!

How do athletes stay cool during a game?
They stand near the fans.

Which sport is always in trouble?
Bad–minton.

What did the two strings do in the race?
They tied.

AEROBIC AL: Is your refrigerator running?
GREEDY GRAHAM: Yeah.
AEROBIC AL: Well you'd better go catch it.

What time of year do you jump on a trampoline?
Springtime.

When is cricket a crime?
When there's a hit and run.

Where do spiders play football?
Webley.

*What do runners do when they forget
something?*
They jog their memory.

**Now c'mon, you lazy lumps, vote for me! (Then
run up and down the stairs one hundred times.)**

PETER'S PERFECT JOKES

These are the best jokes in the world, and I know you will all love them. Please vote for one of my jokes.
Peter.

What? These are the dumbest jokes ever! Anyone who reads them will get thrown into a snake pit. Do not read unless you want everyone to know you're a toad.

Knock knock.
Who's there?
Ya.
Yahoo!

Knock knock.
Who's there?
Doctor.
Doctor Who?
You just said.

Knock knock.
Who's there?
Leaf.
Leaf who?
Leaf me alone.

These jokes are so lame. Take my advice and skip over them.

How do you make a witch itch?
Take away the W.

What did the traffic light say to the man crossing the road?
Don't look, I'm changing!

Who invented the plane that didn't fly?
The Wrong Brothers.

What did one earthquake say to another?
It's not my fault.

Who writes invisible books?
A ghost writer.

What is a myth?
A female moth.

I said anyone who is not a toad should skip over these 'jokes'.

Knock Knock.
Who's there?
Cats go.
Cats go who?
*No they don't,
they go meow!!!!!!*

Groan.

*What kind of
  underwear do clouds
  wear?*
Thunderwear.

HENRY: What's that terrible, ugly thing on your shoulder?
PETER: Help! What is it?
HENRY: Your head.

Miss Lovely! Henry's being mean to me!
He's adding jokes on my page!

Henry! Cross that joke out immediately.

**But it's a great joke. I'm only
trying to help Peter . . .**

What nut grows on a wall?
A walnut.

What did the wall say to the corner?
Meet you at the ceiling.

Where does Tarzan get his clothes from?
A jungle sale.

You are a toad, you are a toad . . .

Waaaaa! Henry's calling me a toad.

Stop it Henry.

What do you call an overweight pumpkin?
A plumpkin.

**What has three heads, is ugly,
and smells bad?**
**Oops, my mistake, you don't have
three heads!**

Waaaaaa! Miss Lovely! He did it again! He stuck another joke on my page.

What is the best day to go to the beach?
Sunday, of course.

What does a teddy bear put in his house?
Fur-niture.

What city cheats at exams?
Peking.

I guess you must like snake pits. Oh, okay, you didn't read them, you just skipped through them to the end. Phew. You had me worried there for a minute.

BERT'S BEEFY BEASTLY JOKES

PETER: Why did the chicken cross the road?
BERT: I dunno.

That's pathetic, Bert! Remember guys, vote for my pirate jokes!

Where do cows go on a Saturday night?
To the mooooooovies.

What do you get when you cross a rotten egg with a giant gorilla?
King Pong.

I think you get . . . PETER!

Miss Lovely!! Henry's still writing mean things about me in the new joke book.

Stop it, Henry, or no playtime.

Knock knock.
Who's there?
Cows.
Cows who?
Cows say moo, not who.

What do you call a dog that tells time?
A watch dog.

What newspaper do cats read?
Mews of the World.

Why don't baby birds smile?
Would you like it if
your mother fed
you worms all
day?

What's the difference between a bird and a fly?
A bird can fly but a fly can't bird.

*What has an elephant's trunk, a tiger's
stripes, a giraffe's neck, and a baboon's
bottom?*
A zoo.

*What do you get if
you cross an owl
with a skunk?*
A bird that
smells but doesn't
give a hoot.

What happened to the snake with a cold?
She adder viper nose.

What's the best year for kangaroos?
Leap year.

What did the porcupine say to the cactus?
Mummy.

What do you call a three legged donkey?
A wonkey.

What do you give a sick bird?
Tweetment.

What is green and goes dit dot dit dot?
A morse toad.

What do you call a frog spy?
A croak and dagger agent.

Why does an elephant wear plimsolls?
To sneak up on mice.

What has four legs and flies?
A dead horse.

Why did the fly fly?
Because the spider spied her.

What do you get from a pampered cow?
Spoiled milk.

What weighs six tons and wears glass slippers?
Cinder-elephant.

Where do polar bears vote?
The North Poll.

Where was Camelot?
A place where people parked their camels.

What do you get when you cross a lizard and a baby?
A creepy crawler.

What did the spider do on the computer?
Made a website.

What do moths study in school?
Mothomatics.

What card game do crocodiles play?
Snap!

Aren't you going to ask people to vote for you, Bert?

I dunno.

CLARE'S CLEVER JOKES

Not everyone can be as smart as me, but have a go at these clever conundrums. Oh, and please vote for one of my brain teasers.

What is the world's longest word?
Smiles, because there's a mile between the first and second 's'.

Why is the sky so high?
So birds don't bump their heads.

What do you get when you cross a pair of pants with a dictionary?
Smarty pants.

When can a donkey be spelled in one letter?
When it's you.

What type of snake is good at sums?
An adder.

Why was 6 afraid of 7?
Because 7 8 9.

What holds the moon up?
Moon beams.

What breaks when you say it?
Silence.

What loses its head in the morning and gets it back at night?
Your pillow.

What's harder to catch the faster you run?
Your breath.

Don't forget to vote for Clever Clare.

BRIAN'S BRAINY RIDDLES

Now come on, all you geniuses out there! Try these riddles, and then show how brainy you are by voting for me.

What's bigger when it's upside down?
The number 6.

What has a mouth, and a fork, but never eats?
A river.

What's in the middle of Paris?
R.

How many sides has a circle got?
Two – the inside and the outside.

What's black when clean and white when dirty?
A blackboard.

What has a tail and a head but no body?
A coin.

What room has no sides, no walls, no doors, and no ceilings?
A mushroom.

What gets wet as it dries?
A towel.

What has two hands and no fingers?
A clock.

What starts with a T, ends with a T, and is full of tea?
A teapot.

What asks no questions, but demands an answer?
The doorbell.

Twelve pears hanging high, twelve men passing by, each took a pear and left eleven hanging there. How can this be?
How can eleven pears be left?
'Each' is a man's name!

Brian is a brain!
Vote Brainy
Brian.

HENRY'S PURPLE HAND PIRATE JOKES

Okay everybody, finally, you are now going to read the best jokes in the book!! Can I help it if mine are so much better than everyone else's? Get your pencils ready to vote . . . Henry!

Why are pirates called pirates?
Because they aaarrrrr!

What does a pirate smoke?
A cigaaaarrrrrr!

What does a pirate's dog say?
Aaaarrrrrf!

What do pirates get on their pizzas?
Arrrrrrtichokes!

What does a Dyslexic Pirate Say?
RRRRAAAAAAAAAA!

Where do Pirates hate to be kicked?
In the ARRRse!

Why does a pirate's phone go beep beep beep beep beep?
Because he left it off the hook.

What's a pirate's favourite letter?
P. Because it's an R, but it's missing a leg!

What do you get when you cross a pirate with Santa Claus?
Yo ho ho ho!

What has 8 legs, 8 arms and 8 eyes?
8 pirates.

How much do pirates pay for their earrings?
A buccaneer.

Why did Captain Hook cross the road?
To get to the second hand shop.

**Remember: vote often, for . . .
Henry!!**

HORRID HENRY'S LAST LAUGH

Shh, don't tell, I've sneaked in a few practical jokes. Don't let Miss Battle-Axe know!!!!!

1) Did you know that if you mix shampoo with grass and leave it on the floor, Mum and Dad will think the cat threw up?

2) Carry a piece of old cloth with you. Wait till your victim sits down or bends over, then rip it behind their back. They will be so embarrassed!!!

3) Don't forget about putting salt in the sugar bowl . . .

4) Want to give your yucky sister or revolting brother a fright? One weekend, move their clock ahead three hours. When they wake up, they'll think they over-slept!

5) Psst, here's a quick way to make some cash. Tell your silly sister or brother: 'Bet you I can push myself under the door.' When they accept the bet, write MYSELF on a piece of paper and push it under the door. Collect your well-earned cash!

6) Ask your horrible, smelly brother or sister:

If frozen water is iced water, and frozen lemonade is iced lemonade, what's frozen ink?

Visit Horrid Henry's website at
www.horridhenry.co.uk for competitions, games,
downloads and a monthly newsletter!

SEND HENRY YOUR FAVOURITE JOKE.

Postcards to:

Horrid Henry,
c/o Orion Children's Books,
5 Upper St Martin's Lane,
London WC2H 9EA.

Make sure you sign your full name, because if your joke is used in a future joke book, we'll print your name in the book!

HORRID HENRY BOOKS

Visit Horrid Henry's website at www.horridhenry.co.uk for competitions, games, downloads and a monthly newsletter!